Books by Mark Strand

LOOKING FOR POETRY

3

LOOKING FOR POETRY

Poems by Carlos Drummond de Andrade
and Rafael Alberti

and

Songs from the Quechua

Translated by MARK STRAND

Alfred A. Knopf

NEW YORK • 2002

This Is a Borzoi Book
Published by Alfred A. Knopf

www.randomhouse.com/knopf/poetry

Library of Congress Cataloging-in-Publication Data
Looking for poetry : poems by Carlos Drummond de
Andrade and Rafael Alberti and songs from the Quechua / translated
by Mark Strand.—1st ed.
p. cm.
Poems from previously published collections.
ISBN 0-375-70988-6 (alk. paper)
1. Andrade, Carlos Drummond de, 1902–1987. Translations
into English. 2. Alberti, Rafael, 1902–1999. Translations into
English. I. Strand, Mark II. Andrade, Carlos Drummond de,
1902–1987. Poems. English. Selections. III. Alberti, Rafael,
1902–1999. Poems. English. Selections.
PQ9697.A7185 A267 2002
869.1'41—dc21 2001038518

Manufactured in the United States of America
First Edition

Contents

Poems by Carlos Drummond de Andrade

Songs from the Quechua

Poems by Rafael Alberti

Poems by Carlos Drummond de Andrade

Note to the Poetry of
Carlos Drummond de Andrade

Carlos Drummond de Andrade, one of the most revered Brazilian poets of the twentieth century, was born in 1902 in Itabira, a small mining town in the Brazilian state of Minas Gerais. He died in Rio de Janeiro in 1987. His poems are, for the most part, bittersweet evocations of a small-town childhood or, more emblematically, remorseful accounts of a lost world or simply discreet and sometimes ironic views of the way things are. Though they seem to concern themselves with the ubiquity of loss, they are often amusing. So easily do humor and seriousness coexist in Drummond's work that their unexpected harmony may account in part for his popularity. This harmony is evident even in his city poems, where the balance is tipped toward seriousness, and where the reader is made to feel that life is a forced march and all any of us can do is endure it. Even in these, despite their litanies of ills, one feels the presence of humor and of a forgiving lightness that reveals, at the least, the poet's unusual capacity for sympathizing.

Like other poets of his period, Drummond's poetic loyalty was with Modernism. This meant turning his back on the inflated rhetoric of Symbolism and Parnassianism and adopting a rhetoric of his own, one that was plainer, and flexible enough to respond to the rapid changes around him. In Brazil these changes had largely to do with the shift from the old agricultural aristocracy to the quickly growing industrial class. It is easy to witness in Drummond's poems these two worlds in conflict. It is just as easy to see that what the twentieth century demanded was not just severance from the past but an alarming and sometimes desperate need to keep up with the present.

Despite Drummond's aesthetic allegiance, he nevertheless held on to elements commonly associated with traditional lyric poetry. His most famous poem, "In the Middle of the Road," which first appeared in 1928, created an immediate sensation, some readers deeming it rubbish, others finding it stunningly original. What it ends up being is a very simple poem whose power depends on the incantatory repetition of the first line and the admission or promise that what it records will never be forgotten. It insists on the value of an event or an image that by any measure would be insignificant. It suggests that a poet should be responsible to all of what the world offers him. But, as in many Drummond poems, this one hangs in the balance between seriousness and humor. There is something outrageous about the claims this poem makes in its memorializing, and yet it enacts one of the central concerns of lyric poetry—to rescue from oblivion as much of our human experience as we can.

Seven-Sided Poem

When I was born, one of those
crooked angels who live in shadow
said: Go on, Carlos, be *gauche* in life.

The houses look out on men
chasing after women.
If the afternoon were blue
there might be less desire.

The trolley passes full of legs:
white, black, yellow legs.
My God, my heart asks, why so many legs.
But my eyes
ask nothing.

The man behind the mustache
is serious, simple, and strong.
He hardly talks.
He has few and precious friends,
the man behind the glasses and the mustache.

My God, why hast Thou forsaken me.
Thou knewest I wasn't God
Thou knewest how weak I was.

World, wide world,
if my name were Harold
it might be a rhyme
but no answer.
World, wide world,

my heart is bigger
than you are.

I shouldn't tell you
but this moon
and this cognac
are hell on a person's feelings.

In the Middle of the Road

In the middle of the road there was a stone
there was a stone in the middle of the road
there was a stone
in the middle of the road there was a stone.

I'll never forget this event
in the lifetime of my tired eyes.
I'll never forget that in the middle of the road
there was a stone
there was a stone in the middle of the road
in the middle of the road there was a stone.

Quadrille

John loved Teresa who loved Raymond
who loved Mary who loved Jack who loved Lily
who didn't love anybody.
John went to the United States, Teresa to a convent
Raymond died in an accident, Mary became an old maid,
Jack committed suicide and Lily married J. Pinto Fernandez
who didn't figure into the story.

The Onset of Love

The hammock between two mango trees
swayed in the sunken world.
It was hot, windless.
Above was the sun,
between were leaves.
It was broiling.

And since I had nothing to do, I developed a passion for the legs of the
  laundress.

One day she came to the hammock,
curled up in my arms,
gave me a hug,
gave me her breasts
that were just for me.
The hammock turned over,
down went the world.

And I went to bed
with a fever of forty degrees.
And a giant laundress with giant breasts was spinning around in the
  greenness of space.

Ballad of Love Through the Ages

From the beginning of time,
I liked you, you liked me.
I was Greek, you were Trojan,
Trojan but not Helen.
I sprung from a wooden horse
to kill your brother.
I killed, we quarrelled, we died.

I became a Roman soldier,
persecutor of Christians.
At the catacomb door
I met you again.
But when I saw you fall
naked in the Colosseum
and the lion coming toward you,
I made a desperate leap
and the lion ate us both.

Next I was a Moorish pirate,
the scourge of Tripoli.
I set fire to the frigate
where you were hiding from
the fury of my brigantine.
But when I went to grab you
and take you as my slave,
you crossed yourself and drove
a dagger through your heart.
I killed myself as well.

Later on, in happier days,
I was a courtier at Versailles,
clever and debauched.
You dreamed of being a nun . . .
I vaulted over the convent wall
but difficult politics
led us to the guillotine.

These days I'm totally modern:
dancing, jogging, working out.
And I have money in the bank.
And you're a fabulous blonde:
dancing, jogging, working out.
None of it pleases your father.
But after a thousand reversals,
I, one of Paramount's heroes,
give you a hug, a kiss, and we marry.

Dawn

The poet rode the trolley drunk.
The sun came up behind the yards.
The small hotels slept very sadly.
The houses too were drunk.

Everything was a total wreck.
Nobody knew that the world was going to end
(only a child did but kept it quiet),
that the world was going to end at 7:45.
Last thoughts! Last telegrams!

Joe who listed pronouns,
Helen who loved men,
Sebastian who ruined himself,
Arthur who never said anything,
set off for eternity.

The poet is drunk, but
he hears a voice in the dawn:
Why don't we all go dancing
between the trolley and the tree?

Between the trolley and the tree
dance, brothers!
Even without music
dance, brothers!
Children are being born
with so much spontaneity.
Love is fantastic
(love and what it produces).

Dance, brothers!
Death will come later
like a sacrament.

Don't Kill Yourself

Carlos, calm down, love
is what you are seeing:
a kiss today, tomorrow no kiss,
the day after tomorrow is Sunday
and nobody knows what will happen
on Monday.

It's useless to resist
or to commit suicide.
Don't kill yourself. Don't kill yourself.
Save all of yourself for the wedding
though nobody knows when or if
it will ever come.

Carlos, earthy Carlos, love
spent the night with you
and your most hidden self
is raising a terrible racket,
prayers,
victrolas,
saints in procession,
ads for the best soap,
it is a racket for which nobody knows
the why or wherefore.

Meanwhile you walk
upright, unhappy.
You are the palm tree, you are the shout
nobody heard in the theater
and all the lights went out.

Love in darkness, no, in daylight,
is always sad, Carlos my boy,
but don't tell anyone,
nobody knows or will know.

Song of the Phantom Girl of Belo Horizonte

I am the phantom girl
who waits on Chumbo Street
for the coach of dawn.
I am white and tall and cold,
my flesh is a sigh
in the mountain dawn.
I am the phantom girl.
My name was Maria,
Maria-Who-Died.

I am the girl you loved
who died of sickness,
who died in a car crash,
who killed herself on the beach,
whose hair stayed
long in your memory.
I was never of this world:
when kissed, my mouth
spoke of other planets
where lovers burn
in a chaste fire
and without irony
turn into stars.

Unlike the others, I died
without having time to be yours.
I cannot get used to this,
and when the police are asleep
in and around me,
my wandering ghost

goes down Curral Hill,
spying on the new houses,
circling the lovers' gardens
(Cláudio Manuel da Costa Street),
stopping for shelter in the Hotel Ceará
that offers no shelter. A perfume
I do not know invades me:
it is the odor of your sleep,
soft and warm, curled up
in the arms of Spanish women . . .
Oh! Let me sleep with you!

My ghost keeps going,
for I meet none of my lovers,
who were seduced by French women,
who drank all the whisky
in Brasil
(and are now in a drunken sleep),
and meet only cars that pass
with drivers who, surprised
by my whiteness, flee.
The shy policemen,
poor things! One wanted to grab me.
I opened my arms. . . . Incredulous,
he felt me. There was no flesh
and outside the dress
and under the dress
the same white absence,
a white anguish . . .
It is obvious: what was body
was eaten by the cat.

The girls that are still alive
(they'll die, you can be sure)

are afraid that I'll appear
and pull them down by their legs . . .
    They're wrong.
I was a girl, I will be a girl
deserted, *per omnia saecula.*
I have no interest in girls.
Boys disturb me.
I don't know how to free myself.
If only my ghost wouldn't suffer,
if only they would still like me.
If only the spirit would consent,
but I know it's forbidden,
you are flesh, I am mist.

A mist that dissolves
when the sun breaks in the mountains.

Now I feel better,
I've said everything I wanted to,
I would climb that cloud,
be a frozen sheet
sparkling over mankind.
But the stars will not understand,
nobody will understand,
my reflection in the pool
on Paráuna Avenue.

Boy Crying in the Night

In the warm, humid night, noiseless and dead, a boy cries.
His crying behind the wall, the light behind the window
are lost in the shadow of muffled footsteps, of tired voices.
Yet the sound of medicine poured into a spoon can be heard.

A boy cries in the night, behind the wall, across the street,
far away a boy cries, in another city,
in another world, perhaps.

And I see the hand that lifts the spoon while the other holds the head,
and I see the slick thread run down the boy's chin,
and slip into the street, only a thread, and slip through the city.
And nobody else in the world exists but that boy crying.

The Dead in Frock Coats

In the corner of the living room was an album of unbearable photos,
many meters high and infinite minutes old,
over which everyone leaned
making fun of the dead in frock coats.

Then a worm began to chew the indifferent coats,
the pages, the inscriptions, and even the dust on the pictures.
The only thing it did not chew was the everlasting sob of life that
        broke
and broke from those pages.

Your Shoulders Hold Up the World

A time comes when you no longer can say: my God.
A time of total cleaning up.
A time when you no longer can say: my love.
Because love proved useless.
And the eyes don't cry.
And the hands do only rough work.
And the heart is dry.

Women knock at your door in vain, you won't open.
You remain alone, the light turned off,
and your enormous eyes shine in the dark.
It is obvious you no longer know how to suffer.
And you want nothing from your friends.

Who cares if old age comes, what is old age?
Your shoulders are holding up the world
and it's lighter than a child's hand.
Wars, famine, family fights inside buildings
prove only that life goes on
and not everybody has freed himself yet.
Some (the delicate ones) judging the spectacle cruel
will prefer to die.
A time comes when death doesn't help.
A time comes when life is an order.
Just life, without any escapes.

Souvenir of the Ancient World

Clara strolled in the garden with the children.
The sky was green over the grass,
the water was golden under the bridges,
other elements were blue and rose and orange,
a policeman smiled, bicycles passed,
a girl stepped onto the lawn to catch a bird,
the whole world—Germany, China—
    all was quiet around Clara.

The children looked at the sky: it was not forbidden.
Mouth, nose, eyes were open. There was no danger.
What Clara feared were the flu, the heat, the insects.
Clara feared missing the eleven o'clock trolley:
She waited for letters slow to arrive,
She couldn't always wear a new dress. But she strolled in the garden,
    in the morning!
They had gardens, they had mornings in those days!

Motionless Faces

Father dead, loved one dead.
Aunt dead, brother born dead.
Cousins dead, friend dead.
Grandfather dead, mother dead
(hands white, portrait on the wall always crooked, speck of dust in
    the eyes).
Acquaintances dead, teacher dead.

Enemy dead.

Fiancée dead, girl friends dead.
Engineer dead, passenger dead.
Unrecognizable body dead: a man's? an animal's?
Dog dead, bird dead.
Rosebush dead, orange trees dead.
Air dead, bay dead.
Hope, patience, eyes, sleep, movement of hands: dead.

Man dead. Lights go on.
He works at night as if he were living.

Good morning! He is stronger (as if he were living).

Dead without an obituary, secretly dead.
He knows how to imitate hunger, and how to pretend to love.

And how to insist on walking, and how well he walks.
He could walk through walls, but he uses doors.

His pale hand says goodbye to Russia.
Time enters and leaves him endlessly.

The dead pass quickly; they cannot be held on to.
As soon as one leaves, another one is tapping your shoulder.
I woke up and saw the city:
the dead were like machines,
the houses belonged to the dead,
drowsy waves,
an exhausted chest smelling of lilies,
feet bound up.
I slept and went to the city:
everything was burning,
crackling of bamboo,
mouth dry, suddenly puckering.
I dreamt and returned to the city.
But it wasn't the city anymore.
They were all dead, the medical examiner was checking the tags on
    the corpses.
The medical examiner himself had died years ago but his hand
    continued implacably.
The awful stench was everywhere.

From this veranda without a railing I watch both twilights.
I watch my life running away with a wolf's speed, I want to stop it, but
    would I be bitten?
I look at my feet, how they have grown, flies circulate among them.
I look at everything and add it up, nothing is left, I am poor, poor,
    poor,
but I cannot enter the circle,
I cannot remain alone,
I shall kiss everyone on the forehead,
I shall distribute moist flowers,
after . . . There is no after or before.
There is cold on all sides,
and a central cold, whiter still.

Colder still . . .
A whiteness that pays well our old anger and bitterness . . .
Feeling myself so clear among you, kissing you and getting no dust in
    my mouth or face.
Peace of wispy trees,
of fragile mountains down below, of timid riverbanks, of gestures that
    can no longer annoy,
sweet peace without eyes, in the dark, in the air.
Sweet peace within me,
within my family that came from a fog unbroken by the sun
and returns to their islands by underground roads,
in my street, in my time—finally—reconciled,
in the city of my birth, in my rented rooms,
in my life, in everyone's life, in the mild and deep death of myself and
    everyone.

José

What now, José?
The party's over,
the lights are out,
the people are gone,
the night is cold,
what now, José?
what do you say?
nameless José,
who teases others,
who makes up verses,
who loves? Who quarrels?
what now, José?

You have no woman,
you've run out of words,
you've run out of love,
you can't drink anymore,
you can't smoke anymore,
you can't even spit,
the night is cold,
the day's not come,
the trolley's not come,
not come is utopia
and nobody's laughing
and everything's over
and everything's gone
and everything's stale,
what now José?

What now, José?
Your sweet talk,
your feasting and fasting,
your moment of fever,
your books,
your gold mines,
your suit of glass,
your incoherence,
your anger—what now?

The key's in your hand,
you want to open the door,
there is no door;
you want to die in the sea,
the sea dried up;
you want to go to Minas,
Minas is gone;
José, what now?

If you screamed,
if you wailed,
if you played
a Vienna waltz,
if you slept,
if you tired,
if you died . . .
But you won't,
you're tough, José!

Alone in the dark
like a wild animal,
without a theogony,
without a bare wall
to lean on,

without a black horse
to ride off on,
you march, José!
But where, José?

The Dirty Hand

My hand is dirty.
I must cut it off.
To wash it is pointless.
The water is putrid.
The soap is bad.
It won't lather.
The hand is dirty.
It's been dirty for years.

I used to keep it
out of sight,
in my pants pocket.
No one suspected a thing.
People came up to me,
wanting to shake hands.
I would refuse,
and the hidden hand
would leave its imprint
on my thigh.
And I saw
it was the same
if I used it or not.
Disgust was the same.

How many nights
in the depths of the house
I washed that hand,
scrubbed it, polished it,
dreamed it would turn
to diamond or crystal

or even, at last,
into a plain white hand,
the clean hand of a man,
that you could shake,
or kiss, or hold
in one of those moments
when two people confess
without saying a word . . .
Only to have
the incurable hand
open its dirty fingers.

And the dirt was vile.
It was not mud or soot
or the caked filth
of an old scab
or the sweat
of a laborer's shirt.
It was a sad dirt
made of sickness
and human anguish.
It was not black;
black is pure.
It was dull,
a dull grayish dirt.
It is impossible
to live with this
gross hand that lies
on the table.
Quick! Cut it off!
Chop it to pieces
and throw it
into the ocean.
With time, with hope

and its intricate workings
another hand will come,
pure, transparent as glass,
and fasten itself to my arm.

Looking for Poetry

Don't write poems about what's happening.
Nothing is born or dies in poetry's presence.
Next to it, life is a static sun
without warmth or light.
Friendships, birthdays, personal matters don't count.
Don't write poems with the body,
that excellent, whole, and comfortable body objects to lyrical
      outpouring.
Your anger, your grimace of pleasure or pain in the dark
mean nothing.
Don't show off your feelings
that are slow in coming around and take advantage of doubt.
What you think and feel are not poetry yet.

Don't sing about your city, leave it in peace.
Song is not the movement of machines or the secret of houses.
It is not music heard in passing, noise of the sea in streets that skirt the
      borders of foam.
Song is not nature
or men in society.
Rain and night, fatigue and hope, mean nothing to it.
Poetry (you don't get it from things)
leaves out subject and object.

Don't dramatize, don't invoke,
don't question, don't waste time lying.
Don't get upset.
Your ivory yacht, your diamond shoe,
your mazurkas and tirades, your family skeletons,
all of them worthless, disappear in the curve of time.

Don't bring up
your sad and buried childhood.
Don't waver between the mirror
and a fading memory.
What faded was not poetry.
What broke was not crystal.

Enter the kingdom of words as if you were deaf.
Poems are there that want to be written.
They are dormant, but don't be let down,
their virginal surfaces are fresh and serene.
They are alone and mute, in dictionary condition.
Live with your poems before you write them.
If they're vague, be patient. If they offend, be calm.
Wait until each one comes into its own and demolishes
with its command of words
and its command of silence.
Don't force poems to let go of limbo.
Don't pick up lost poems from the ground.
Don't fawn over poems. Accept them
as you would their final and definitive form,
distilled in space.

Come close and consider the words.
With a plain face hiding thousands of other faces
and with no interest in your response,
whether weak or strong,
each word asks:
Did you bring the key?

Take note:
words hide in the night
in caves of music and image.
Still humid and pregnant with sleep
they turn in a winding river and by neglect are transformed.

Carlos Drummond de Andrade   *33*

In the Golden Age

In the golden age
the road was all.
On the right side
were gardens
we would enter
only to exit
on the left,
the left was always
guarded by fences.
This would happen
a thousand times.

For the room
to be elsewhere
only a candle was needed.
Our faces were
buried in books
forever it seemed.
And the key to the cellar
was ours, like the un-
forgettable girl
of the waterfall,
bathing within us,
space and vision
were multiplied
in the golden age.

In the golden age
that was really copper
there were many nights

of pouring rain.
An awful palm
fed up with the city
went to the jungle.
And after the mail
came the assassin.
Africa's wealth
was lost in the wind.
And it was hard
to be a young boy.

Just on the verge
of modern times,
we were held up
while gardens
of sickness,
streetcars of boredom,
stores of tears,
all prospered.
Space is small.
Things pile up.
And making the rounds,
from hand to hand
goes a sealed
white paper,
the plan, perhaps,
of the golden age.

In the golden age
that sleeps on the floor
about to wake up,
I tried to discover
distant roads,
early rivers,

genuine trust,
and superlative poems.
Whenever it's asked
that these things be explained
I haven't the strength.
The trick is to wait.

In the golden age
my heart smiling,
my eyes like diamonds,
my lips keeping time
to some pure song.
In the town market
I sense the new clothes
and I hear the flags
spill out on the air.

In the golden age
childhood comes back
in return for nothing
and space reopened
allows to vanish
the smallest men,
the brittlest things,
the needle, the trip,
the mouth's color,
allows to vanish
the oil of things,
allows to vanish
Saturdays' lawns,
allows to vanish
the paralytic dog,
allows to vanish
my sweetheart,

allows to vanish
the circle of water
reflecting the face . . .
Allows to vanish
the dull cloth,
holding her so
in the golden age.

Residue

From everything a little remained.
From my fear. From your disgust.
From stifled cries. From the rose
a little remained.

A little remained of light
caught inside the hat.
In the eyes of the pimp
a little remained of tenderness,
very little.

A little remained of the dust
that covered your white shoes.
Of your clothes a little remained,
a few velvet rags, very
very few.

From everything a little remained.
From the bombed-out bridge,
from the two blades of grass,
from the empty pack
of cigarettes a little remained.

So from everything a little remains.
A little remains of your chin
in the chin of your daughter.

A little remained of your
blunt silence, a little
in the angry wall,
in the mute rising leaves.

A little remained from everything
in porcelain saucers,
in the broken dragon, in the white flowers,
in the creases of your brow,
in the portrait.

Since from everything a little remains,
why won't a little
of me remain? In the train
travelling north, in the ship,
in newspaper ads,
why not a little of me in London,
a little of me somewhere?
In a consonant?
In a well?

A little remains dangling
in the mouths of rivers,
just a little, and the fish
don't avoid it, which is very unusual.

From everything a little remains.
Not much: this absurd drop
dripping from the faucet,
half salt and half alcohol,
this frog leg jumping,
this watch crystal
broken into a thousand wishes,
this swan's neck,
this childhood secret . . .
From everything a little remained:
from me; from you; from Abelard.
Hair on my sleeve,
from everything a little remained;

wind in my ears,
burbing, rumbling
from an upset stomach,
and small artifacts:
bell jar, honeycomb, revolver
cartridge, aspirin tablet.
From everything a little remained.

And from everything a little remains.
Oh, open the bottles of lotion
and smother
the cruel, unbearable odor of memory.

Still, horribly, from everything a little remains,
under the rhythmic waves
under the clouds and the wind
under the bridges and under the tunnels
under the flames and under the sarcasm
under the phlegm and under the vomit
under the cry from the dungeon, the guy they forgot
under the spectacles and under the scarlet death
under the libraries, asylums, victorious churches
under yourself and under your feet already hard
under the ties of family, the ties of class,
from everything a little always remains.
Sometimes a button. Sometimes a rat.

Story of the Dress

Mother, whose dress is hanging
there on that nail?

Children, that is the dress
of a woman who is gone.

When did she go, Mother?
When did we know her?

Hold your tongues, children,
your father is coming.

Mother, say quickly
whose dress is that dress.

Children, her body is cold
and does not wear clothes.

The dress on that nail
is lifeless, is calm.

Listen, children,
to the words that I say.

There once was a woman
your father was mad for.

He was so much in love
that we could not reach him,

he cut himself off,
shut himself up,

devoured himself,
cried on the meat platter,

drank and quarrelled,
and beat me up,

he left me behind with your cradle,
went to that woman,

but she didn't care.
Your father begged, but so what?

He gave her insurance, a farm,
gave her a car, gave her gold,

he would lap up her leavings,
would lick her shoes.

But she didn't care.
Your furious father

then asked me to ask
that devilish woman

if she would be patient
and sleep with him. . . .

Mother, why are you crying?
Take one of our handkerchiefs.

Children, be still,
your father's in the courtyard.

Mother, none of us heard
his foot on the stairs.

Children, I searched all over
for that demon-woman.

I begged her to yield
to my husband's will.

I don't love your husband,
she said with a laugh.

But I can stay with him,
if that's what you want,

just to please you, not me,
I don't want a man.

I looked at your father,
his eyes were pleading.

I looked at the woman,
her eyes were happy.

Her fancy dress
with its plunging neckline

showed more than it hid
of her sinner's parts.

I crossed myself,
I bowed . . . I said yes.

I left thinking of death,
but death did not come.

I walked the five streets,
by the bridge, by the river,

I went to your relatives,
did not eat, did not talk,

I had a high fever,
but death did not come.

The danger passed,
my hair had turned white,

I had lost my teeth,
my eyesight was gone,

I took in laundry,
I sewed, I made candy,

my hands were scarred,
my rings were broken,

my gold chain paid
the bill at the pharmacy.

Your father had vanished.
But the world is small.

A woman with nothing but pride
appeared one day,

poor, broken, unfortunate,
holding a package.

Woman, she said in a husky voice,
I'm not returning your husband,

I don't know where he is.
But here's this dress,

the last bit of luxury
that I kept as a keepsake

from that scandalous day,
that day of great shame.

I did not love him,
love came later.

By that time, he was repelled
and said that he liked me

as I used to be.
I threw myself at his feet,

tried every wile,
scraped my face on the floor,

pulled my hair,
hurled myself into the stream,

slashed myself with a penknife,
threw myself into the sewer,

drank down faith and gasoline,
prayed two hundred novenas,

woman, it was useless,
your husband has vanished.

I bring you the clothes
that record my wrongdoing

of hurting a wife,
of trampling her pride.

Please take this dress
and give me your pardon.

I looked at her face,
where were those eyes,

that gracious smile,
that neck of camellia,

that waistline
so comely and slim,

those delicate feet
in satin sandals?

I looked at her hard,
without saying a word.

I took the dress,
and hung it on that nail.

And she stole quickly away
while down the street

your father appeared.
He looked silently at me,

hardly noticed the dress
and said only: Woman,

lay my dish on the table.
I did, he sat down,

he ate, wiped his sweat,
he was always the same,

he ate half sideways
and had not aged.

The sound of food
in his mouth warmed me,

gave me great peace,
an exquisite feeling

that all was a dream,
no dress . . . no nothing.

Children, listen! I hear
your father climbing the stairs.

The Elephant

I make an elephant
from the little
I have. Wood
from old furniture
holds him up, and I fill him
with cotton, silk,
and sweetness.
Glue keeps his heavy
ears in place.
His rolled-up trunk
is the happiest part
of his architecture.
And his tusks are made
of that rare material
I cannot fake.
A white fortune
rolling around
in circus dust
without being
lost or stolen.
And finally there are
the eyes where the most
fluid and permanent
part of the elephant
stays, free of dishonesty.

Here's my poor elephant
ready to leave
to find friends
in a tired world

that no longer believes
in animals and doesn't
trust in things.
Here he is: an imposing
and fragile hulk,
who shakes his head
and moves slowly,
his hide stitched
with cloth flowers
and clouds—allusions
to a more poetic world
where love reassembles
the natural forms.

My elephant goes
down a crowded street,
but nobody looks
not even to laugh
at his tail that threatens
to leave him.
He is all grace, except
his legs don't help
and his swollen belly
will collapse
at the slightest touch.
He expresses
with elegance
his minimal life
and no one in town
is willing to take
to himself
from that tender body
the fugitive image,
the clumsy walk.

Easily moved,
he yearns for
sad situations,
unhappy people,
moonlit encounters
in the deepest ocean,
under the roots of trees,
in the bosom of shells;
he yearns for lights
that don't blind
yet shine through
the thickest trunks.
He walks the battlefield
without crushing plants,
searching for places,
secrets, stories
untold in any book,
whose style only the wind,
the leaves, the ant
recognize, but men
ignore since they dare
show themselves only
under a veiled peace
and to closed eyes.

And now late at night
my elephant returns,
but returns tired out,
his shaky legs
break down in the dust.
He didn't find
what he wanted,
what we wanted,
I and my elephant,

in whom I love
to disguise myself.
Tired of searching,
his huge machinery
collapses like paper.
The paste gives way
and all his contents,
forgiveness, sweetness,
feathers, cotton,
burst out on the rug,
like a myth torn apart.
Tomorrow I begin again.

Death in a Plane

I awaken for death.
I shave, dress, put on my shoes.
It is my last day: a day
not broken by one premonition.
Everything happens as usual.
I head for the street. I am going to die.

I shall not die now. A whole day
unfolds before me.
What a long day it is! And in the street
what a lot of steps I take! And what a lot of things
have accumulated in time! Without paying much attention
I keep on going. So many faces
crowded into a notebook!

I visit the bank. What good
is the money, if a few hours later
the police come and take it
from the hole that was my chest?
But I don't see myself wounded and bloody.
I am clean, spotless, bright, summery.
Nevertheless, I walk toward death.
I walk into offices, into mirrors
into hands that are offered, into eyes
that are nearsighted, into mouths that smile or simply talk.
I do not say goodbye, I know nothing, I am not afraid:
death hides
its breath and its strategy.

I lunch. What for? I eat a fish in a sauce of gold and cream.
It is my last fish on my last
fork. The mouth distinguishes, chooses, decides,
swallows. Music passes through the sweets, a shiver
from a violin or the wind, I don't know. It isn't death.
It is the sun. The crowded trolleys. Work.
I am in a great city and I am a man
in a cogwheel. I am in a rush. I am going to die.
I ask the slow ones to clear a path for me. I don't look
at the cafés rattling with coffee cups and conversation.
I don't look at the shaded wall of the old hospital.
Nor at the posters. I am in a rush. I buy a paper. It's a rush
even if it means death!

The day already come around to its midpoint does not tell me
that I too have begun to come to an end. I am tired.
I want to sleep, but the preparations. The telephone.
The bills. The letters. I do a thousand things
that will create another thousand, here, there, in the United States.
I'll do anything. I make dates
that I shall never keep, I utter words in vain.
I lie, saying: "Until tomorrow." But tomorrow won't be.

I decline with the afternoon, my head aches, I defend myself,
hand myself a pill: at least
the water drowns what hurts,
the fly, the buzzing . . . but nothing I will die from: death cheats,
cheats like a soccer player,
chooses like a cashier,
carefully, among illnesses and disasters.

Still it isn't death, it is the shadow
over tired buildings, the interval between
two races. Heavy business slows down,

engineers, executives, laborers, are finishing up.
But cabdrivers, waiters, and a thousand other
nighttime workers are getting started. The city
changes hands.

I go home. Again I clean up.
So my hair will be neat
and my nails not bring to mind the rebellious child of long ago.
The clothes without dust. The plastic suitcase.
I lock up my room. I lock up my life.
The elevator locks me up. I am calm.

For the last time I look at the city.
I can still turn back, put off death,
not take that car. Not go.
I can turn and say: "Friends,
I forgot a paper, there's no trip."
Then go to the casino, read a book.

But I take the car. I point out the place
where something is waiting. The field. Searchlights.
I pass by marble, glass, chrome.
I climb some steps. I bend. I enter
death's interior.

Death arranges seats to make the wait
more comfortable. Here one meets
those who are going to die and do not know it.
Newspapers, coffee, chewing gum, cotton for the ear,
small services daintily surround
our strapped-in bodies.
We are going to die, it is not only
my single and limited death,
twenty of us will be destroyed,

twenty of us will die,
twenty of us will be smashed to bits, and right now.

Or almost now. First the private,
personal, silent death of the individual.
I die secretly and without pain,
to live only as a piece of twenty,
and in me incorporate all the pieces
of those who are silently dying as I am.
All of us are one in twenty, a bouquet
of vigorous breaths about to be blown apart.

And we hang,
coldly we hang over the loves
and business of the country.
Toy streets disappear,
lights dim, hills dissolve,
there is only a mattress of clouds,
only a cold oxygen tube grazes my ears,
a tube that is sealed: and inside
the illumined and lukewarm body we live
in comfort and solitude, quiet and nothingness.

So smooth in the night is this machine and so easily does it cut
through increasingly larger blocks of air
that I live
my final moment and it's as if
I had been living for years
before and after today
a continuous and indomitable life
where there were no pauses, lapses, dreams.

I am twenty in the machine
that purrs softly

between starry pictures and the remote breaths of earth,
I feel at home thousands of meters high,
neither bird, nor myth,
I take stock of my powers,
and I fly without mystery,
a body flying, holding onto pockets, watches, nails,
tied to the earth by memory and muscular habit,
flesh soon to explode.

Oh, whiteness, serenity under the violence
of death without previous notice,
careful despite the unavoidable closeness
of atmospheric danger,
a shattering blast of air, splinter of wind
on the neck, lightning
flash burst crack
broken we tumble
straight down I fall and am turned into news.

Interpretation of December

Maybe it's the child
suspended in memory.
Two lit candles
in the depths of the room.
And the Jewish face
in the print, maybe.
The smell of various burners
under each pot.
Holy feet walking
in snow, in the backlands,
in the imagination.

The doll broken
before it was played with,
also a wheel
in the garden somewhere,
and the iron train
passing over me
so lightly: It doesn't crush me,
but remembers me instead.

It is the letter written
with difficult letters,
mailed at a post office
without stamp or approval.
The open window
where wandering eyes
lean out,
eyes that ask
and don't know how to give.

The old man sleeping
in the wrong chair.
The torn newspaper.
The dog pointing.
The cockroach scurrying.
The smell of cake.
The wind blowing.
And the clock stopped.

More litany of the mass
than can be suppressed,
the white dress
in a white street
flying back to the cold.
The hidden sweetness,
the forbidden book,
the frustrated bath,
the failed victory,
the dream of dancing
over a floor of water
or that voyage upon
the vastness of time
where the oldest laws
are never reached.

It is loneliness
in front of the chestnut trees,
the dull zone
in the sphere of sound,
the wine stain
in the drunken towel,
displeasure of five hundred
mouths swallowing
false candy

still moist
from the weeping of streets.

The empty hut
in the land without music.
The shared silence
in the land of ants.
The sleep of lizards
that never hear the bell.
Talk of fish
about things liquid.
Stories of the spider
at war with mosquitoes.
Stains of cut
and rotten wood.
Stinginess of stone
in a dull monologue.
The mine of mica
and the figurehead.
The natural night
without enchantment.
Something irreducible
in the life-giving legends
yet incorporated
in the heart of myth.

It is the child within us
or outside us
harvesting myth.

An Ox Looks at Man

They are more delicate even than shrubs and they run
and run from one side to the other, always forgetting
something. Surely they lack I don't know what
basic ingredient, though they present themselves
as noble or serious, at times. Oh, terribly serious,
even tragic. Poor things, one would say that they hear
neither the song of air nor the secrets of hay;
likewise they seem not to see what is visible
and common to each of us, in space. And they are sad,
and in the wake of sadness they come to cruelty.
All their expression lives in their eyes—and loses itself
to a simple lowering of lids, to a shadow.
And since there is little of the mountain about them—
nothing in the hair or in the terribly fragile limbs
but coldness and secrecy—it is impossible for them
to settle themselves into forms that are calm, lasting,
and necessary. They have, perhaps, a kind
of melancholy grace (one minute) and with this they allow
themselves to forget the problems and translucent
inner emptiness that make them so poor and so lacking
when it comes to uttering silly and painful sounds: desire, love,
     jealousy
(what do we know?)—sounds that scatter and fall in the field
like troubled stones and burn the herbs and the water,
and after this it is hard to keep chewing away at our truth.

Song for a Young Girl's Album

Good morning: I said to the girl
who smiled from far away.
Good morning: but she didn't
respond from the distance.
Eye contact was pointless
so I waved my arms
good morning to the girl who,
day or night,
was far out of my range,
far from my poor good morning.
Good morning forever: maybe
the answer will come cold
or come late, yet
I shall wait
for her good morning.
And over the rows of houses,
over the hills and valleys,
I shall lamely repeat
at whatever hour: good morning.
Maybe the time is wrong
and my sadness too great
to warrant
this absurd good morning.
The girl does not know,
or sense, or suspect
the tenderness within
the heart of my good morning.
Good morning: I repeat
in the afternoon;
at midnight: good morning.

And at dawn
I color my day
blue and pink:
so the girl can find it!
good morning.
Good morning: only an echo
in the bushes (but who can say)
makes out my message
or wishes me good morning.
Smiling from far away,
the girl in her joy
does not feel the violence
in the radiance of this
good morning.
Night that had betrayed
sadness, trouble, confusion,
wanders without fire
in the wildest nostalgia.
If only she would say
good morning to my good morning,
the night would change
to the clearest of days!

Encounter

In time I lost my father, in dreams I get him back.
Whenever the night gives me the power to leave,
I feel him again and set my gaze
upon him, and line by line I read his face.

So what if he's dead. The dawn comes
and his face, neither sad nor happy
is the same old face. In the calm
of my dreams he wipes no sweat from his brow.

O my architect and farmer father!
He builds his houses of silence, and his gardens
of ash are ripe; they are watered

by a river flowing all the time
and even beyond time, while in
a single breath our own poor streams go dry.

Songs from the Quechua

Note to the Quechua Poems

When I translated these poems over thirty years ago, I worked from Spanish translations. The Quechuas, who live on the altiplano of Peru and Bolivia, had no written language, which means that the Spanish versions of their poems are in some sense original. The work of taking down what is heard and then transcribing it was undertaken first by priests and later by anthropologists. The attempts to bring into Spanish the folk poetry of the Quechuas has been going on since the mid–nineteenth century and perhaps even earlier. One can find many variations of the same poem, depending on where or when it was first heard. But the important thing about these poems is that their emotional appeal is intact. They are so straightforward and so filled with tenderness that the fact that they exist here twice-removed from their original versions should not be a bar to our enjoyment of them.

To This Song

To this song
you will sleep.
At midnight
I shall come.

The Butterfly Messenger

I asked a butterfly,
I sent a dragonfly,
to go out to see my mother,
to go out to see my father.

The butterfly came back,
the dragonfly came back,
saying, your mother is crying;
saying, your father is suffering.

I went myself,
I took myself there,
and it was true my mother was crying,
and it was true my father was suffering.

Pastoral

I wanted a llama
with a golden coat
bright as the sun,
strong as love,
soft as clouds
unravelled by dawn,
in order to make
a knotted rope
for keeping track
of moons that pass,
of flowers that die.

Song, From Ollantay

Stop, don't eat now,
my little dove,
on the princess's land,
my little dove.
Don't try to eat,
my little dove,
the tempting corn,
my little dove.
The kernels are white,
my little dove,
the ears are still thin,
my little dove.
You won't be nourished,
my little dove,
the leaves are still tender,
my little dove.
Gluttons get caught,
my little dove,
and so will you,
my little dove.
I'm picking a quarrel,
my little dove,
for your own good,
my little dove.
Look at the quail,
my little dove,
there he hangs,
my little dove.
Ask your heart,
my little dove,

consult your feathers,
my little dove.
He was destroyed,
my little dove,
for pecking grain,
my little dove.
And that's what happens,
my little dove,
to careless birds,
my little dove.

Lovely Woman

Lovely woman, with the beauty-spot on your face,
if you are single, come with me;
if you are married, keep on going;
if you are widowed, we'll see, anything could happen.

Crystalline River

Crystalline river
of willow trees,
of tears
of gold fishes,
of weeping
from tall cliffs,

deep river
of *tara* forests
losing yourself
in the winding abyss,
clattering
in the ravine
where parrots have
their hiding place,

dear river,
carry me away,
away
with my beautiful lover
through the middle of rocks
into the clouds of rain.

The Grass Is Crying

The rain falls on the hills,
the frost stays in the fields.
The rain passes, the wind blows,
the grass drips with water.

The grass is crying!
Oh, how the eyes cry in a strange village!
The eyes cry like the grass cries
when the rain passes and the wind blows.

When the wind blows the grass bends,
the tall grass of the hills bends
when the wind blows.
Oh, how the heart bends in a strange village!
Like the tall grass when the wind blows.

My Mother Gave Me Life

My mother gave me life
Ay!
in the middle of a rain cloud
Ay!
so I might cry like the rain
Ay!
so I might move like the rain
Ay!
go from door to door
Ay!
like a feather in the air
Ay!

Song

Prince
Because you're a star
    yes
you shine at night
    yes
under the sun's fire
    yes
I'll never see you
    yes

Princess
If I'm a star
    no
open your heart
    no
and under the sun's fire
    no
half-close your eyes
    no

Prince
You seem to call
    yes
only in moonlight
    yes
and when I come near
    yes
you change into snow
    yes

Princess
If I seem to call
      no
please come quickly
      no
if I change into snow
      no
toss me your fire
      no

Prince
When my fire burns you
      yes
you change into dew
      yes
are you the wind
      yes
or are you a dream
      yes

Princess
If you think I am dew
      no
bring your lips near
      no
though I may be a dream
      no
don't ever lose me
      no

I Am Raising a Fly

I am raising a fly
with wings of gold,
I am raising a fly
with burning eyes.

It brings death
in its eyes of fire,
brings death
in its hair of gold,
in its beautiful wings.

I am raising it
in a green bottle;
nobody knows
if it drinks,
nobody knows
if it eats.

It wanders at night
like a star,
and wounds to death
with its glowing red,
with its eyes of fire.

In its eyes of fire
it brings love,
its blood
shines in the night,
the love it brings
in its heart.

Insect of night,
fly of death,
loving it so,
I am raising it
in a green bottle.

And that is all,
that is all.
Nobody knows
if I give it
something to drink,
if I give it
something to eat.

War Song

We shall drink from the traitor's skull,
we shall wear his teeth as a necklace,
of his bones we shall make flutes,
of his skin we shall make a drum;
later, we'll dance.

When You Find Yourself Alone

When you find yourself alone
on the island in the river,
your father won't be there
to call you:
Alau, my daughter!
your mother won't be able
to reach you:
Alau, my daughter!

Only the royal duck
will walk around you
with rain in its eyes,
with tears of blood;
rain in its eyes,
tears of blood.

And even the royal duck
will leave you
when the waves of the river
rise up,
when the waves of the river
fall down.

But then I shall serenade you,
singing:
"Out on the island, out in the storm,
I'll snatch her young heart,
snatch her young heart,
and carry it off."

Not Even Dew

Vicuña of the high plains, deer of the mountains,
tell me if a dove came by,
the one that left her nest,
that forgot her beloved.
Vicuña of the high plains, stag of the mountains,
come look at my eyes full of tears;
she left me like this, with eyes full of tears,
she left me like this, with a wounded heart.
Oh, I hope she gets thirsty on her way,
and doesn't find frost on the high fields,
and doesn't find dew on the grass!
I hope she gets thirsty on all the roads,
the dove that forgot her beloved!

The Fire I Started

The fire I started in the mountains,
the tough straw I lit on the peak,
will be flaming,
will be burning.
Oh, see if the mountain still is in flames!
And if there is fire, go to it, child!
With your innocent tears
put out the fire;
cry over the blaze
and turn it to ash with your innocent tears.

Little Lizard

Oh, little lizard,
little yellow lizard,
what do you want when you come
circling around me?

Ah, little lizard, if you are single
run and dance soon, little lizard;
whirl and jump, little lizard,
oh, little lizard.

If you are single, little lizard,
sing and start laughing, little lizard,
and love me with all you have,
love me, little lizard, love me.

My Treasure

My treasure,
where is it?
I cry for it
at midnight.
I cry for it.
I miss it
all the time.

Going Away

I am supposed to go today,
but I won't, I'll go tomorrow.
You'll see me playing a flute
made of a fly's bone,
my flag will be a spider's web,
my drum the egg of an ant,
and my cap,
my cap will be a hummingbird's nest.

In the Morning

In the morning
drops of water
on the flowers
are tears the moon
cries all night.

Poems by Rafael Alberti

Note to the Poetry of
Rafael Alberti

Alberti is both a difficult and accessible poet. He is endlessly inventive, yet his themes are recognizably simple. One reads him and feels that he is among the most effortless of poets: Gongoristic sonnets seem written with the same ease as Jiménez-like fragments of song, and lamentations with the same energy as celebratory odes. Whatever he does seems touched with originality and grace.

Almost half the poems in this selection come from two books, *Sobre los Angeles* (1929) and *Sermones y Moradas* (1930). They are poems which follow an especially trying period in Alberti's life, a period he refers to despairingly as "a pit of disasters into which I had fallen." Many factors contributed to his sudden collapse—poverty, sickness, family tensions— but the most important seems to have been "an impossible love." He is silent about the details of its failure and says only that it contributed largely to his breakdown and, consequently, to *Sobre los Angeles* and *Sermones y Moradas*. Of his angels, Alberti says:

> And then the angels were revealed to me, not bodily, as the Christian angels of the fine paintings and prints, but as irresistible forces of the spirit, shaped to the most troubled and secret states of my nature. And I set them loose in bands in the world, blind reincarnations of all that was bloody, desolate, agonized, terrible and, at times, good in me and in what surrounded me.

The poems of these two books are a far cry from the early folkloric poems in *Marinero en Tierra* (1925) or the attempts at baroque elegance which make up part of *Cal y Canto* (1929). The vision is more anguished, more central in its mythology, and not as dependent on the nuances of nostalgia or the rhetoric of embellishment and contrivance. In fact, though the tone of the poems varies greatly, from the plain "Song of the Luckless Angel," say, to "Three Memories of Heaven" with its echoes of Becquer's romanticism, or to the insistently mournful "That Burning Horse in the Lost Forests," and though their imagery may strike one as arbitrary, even evasive, they are determinedly immediate and emotional and deal with the survival of the spirit in its many guises.

Survival is also the theme of his book *Retornos de lo Vivo Lejano* (1952), seven poems from which have been included in this selection. Written while Alberti was in exile in Argentina, it is permeated with the sadness of alienation and dominated by tones of resignation and acceptance. In these poems the poet "goes back" to reclaim what was once his, or else the past "comes back" to reclaim him as Lorca does in "The Coming Back of an Assassinated Poet." What survives is a life lived years ago and in another country.

The songs and ballads that conclude this selection of Alberti's poetry are less explicitly nostalgic than the *Retornos*, but, like them, are poems of exile and, in an obvious fashion, are related to the earlier songs of *Marinero en Tierra*. The yearning in those for the Bay of Cádiz is repeated in the later songs and broadened to include all of Spain or, at times, all of what is not immediately present in the poet's experience. They are poems in which the loneliness and isolation of exile are made more poignant by the proximity of escape, which almost always is suggested by rivers or ships—and yet, there is no way back, only further exile. These poems avoid self-pity by proclaiming, often enough, a satisfied acceptance of the facts.

The inclusion of poems based on great film comedians was initially intended to provide comic relief, as was the inclusion of several poems from *Cal y Canto*, but even here, the relief is partial and Alberti remains, almost against his will, an elegist. The comic mourning for Miss X, the grandiose memorializing of Platko (see note on page 173), the losses recorded in the poems about Charlie Chaplin, Harold Lloyd, and Buster Keaton, though absurd, are nevertheless touching in much the same way that the actors were.

The scope of this selection, then, has been determined by an interest in a certain but pervasive aspect of Alberti's work as well as by the translator's limitations. There were poems that could not be done justice to. There were poems that were translated but discarded because they never achieved proper authority in English. This was true of some of the sonnets, the lavishly baroque poems, and a few poems from *13 Bandas y 48 Estrellas* (1936) and *Capital de la Gloria* (1938), poems concerned with American imperialism on the one hand, and the Spanish Civil War on the other. At one point I considered including some poems from *A la Pintura* (1948), but I felt that they lay too far outside the current of this selection, which is made up strictly of elegies, remembrances, and poems of loss and exile.

Alberti's poems number in the thousands. As a consequence, making a selection is a difficult task. These fifty poems are, perforce, a limited sample. I hope, however, that it contains the essential Alberti and that readers unfamiliar with Alberti's work will be moved by its beauty, its strangeness, and its humanity.

Song

The sea. The sea.
The sea. Only the sea!

Father, why did you bring me
to the city?

Why did you dig me up
from the sea?

In dreams, the surf
tugs at my heart
and wants to carry it off.

Father, why did you bring me
here?

Song

The skirt is so white
of the girl who goes to sea!

Child, I hope it is never stained
by the squid's ink!

Your hands are so white, child,
and you don't even sigh as you leave!

Child, I hope they are never stained
by the squid's ink!

Your heart is so white
and your gaze is so white!

Child, I hope they are never stained
by the squid's ink!

Song

The waves, blue walls
of Africa, go and come back.

When they go . . .
Ah, to go with them!

Ah, to come back with them!
When they come back . . .

Song

If my voice dies on land,
take it down to the sea
and leave it on the shore.

Take it down to the sea
and make it captain
of a white man-of-war.

Honor it with
a sailor's medal:
over its heart an anchor,
and on the anchor a star,
and on the star the wind,
and on the wind a sail!

To Miss X, Buried in the West Wind

Miss X, Miss X: 20 years old!

Blouses in windows,
hairdressers
weeping without your hair
—sheared blond fire—

Miss X, hatless Miss X,
rougeless dawn,
alone,
so free,
you,
in the wind!

You never wore earrings.

The dressmakers in white, on their balconies,
forgotten by heaven.
    —Let's see!
    At last!
    What?
     No!
     It was only a bird,
     not you,
     little Miss X.

The bartender, how sad he is!
 (Beer.
 Lemonade.
 Whiskey.

Gin Fizz.)
He painted the bottles black.
And the flags that brightened the bar,
he has painted them black
and hung them all at half-mast.

And the sky won't deliver your messages!

Thirty ships,
forty seaplanes
and a sailboat loaded with oranges,
filling the sea and the clouds with their racket.

Nothing.

Miss X! Where have you gone?
His Majesty, the King of your country doesn't eat.
The King doesn't sleep.
He smokes.
He dies in a car on the coast.

Ministries,
Banks,
Consulates,
Casinos,
Shops,
Parks,
all closed.

And meanwhile, you, in the wind,
"Do your shoes pinch?"
Miss X, of the seas,
"Say, does the draft bother you?"

Ah, Miss X, Miss X, how dull!
I am yawning.
                    Adiós . . .
                                    Goodbye . . .

(Nobody thinks of you anymore. The steel
butterflies
with broken wings
burning the air
settled on the wind's
swaying dahlias.
Electrocuted sun.
Charred moon.
Fear of winter's white bear.

Forbidden.
By order of the Government,
hunting by sea
or by sky is prohibited.

Nobody thinks of you anymore, little Miss X.)

Swimmer

Move, sea,
run, beach,
wind, stop!

Three maritime nations offer me
an iron apple.

The Eiffel Tower throws out a sky
of announcements and telegrams.
Move, sea!
Long live my name in all the hats
on the boulevard!
And my photograph on the bicycle!
Ah!
And my rights to an island in the Seine!

Run, beach!
What will the King of England think?

The House of Lords
flies a squadron in my honor.
The Minister of Air decorates
an Irish star with my name.
And a floating movie house,
all blue, features my life in its lobby.
Ah!
I have powers over a wave in the Thames.

Wind, stop!
What will His Holiness think?

Angels bring rosaries, stamps,
and Vatican lemons
down to the sea.
Archbishops and Cardinals
paint crosses on my tattered bathing suit.
And with one salt-water kiss
the infallible slippers
are ruined.
Ah!
By the walls of the Tiber,
500 thousand plenary indulgences are granted.

Move, sea,
run, beach,
wind, stop!

Platko

(SANTANDER, MAY 20, 1928)

Nobody forgets, Platko,
no nobody, nobody, nobody,
you blond Hungarian bear.

Not the sea
that jumped in front of you without being able to save you.
Not the rain. Not the wind, not even the stiffest wind.

Not the sea, not the wind, Platko,
blond, bloody Platko,
goalkeeper in the dust,
lightning rod.

No, nobody, nobody, nobody.

Blue and white shirts, in the air,
royal shirts,
rival shirts, against you, flying and dragging you with them,
Platko, far-off Platko,
blond Platko beheaded,
tiger burning in the grass of another country. You, a key,
Platko, you, a broken key,
a golden key, fallen before the golden door!

No, nobody, nobody, nobody,
nobody forgets, Platko.

The sky turned its back.
Blue and scarlet shirts blazed
and died without wind.

The sea turned its eyes away,
collapsed and said nothing.
There was bleeding in the buttonholes,
bleeding for you, Platko,
for your Hungarian blood,
for without your blood, your moves, your great saves, your leaps,
the badges were frightened.

No, nobody, nobody, nobody,
nobody, nobody forgets.

It was the sea's return.
There were
ten swift flags
wildly burning.
It was the wind's return.
It was hope's return to the heart.
It was your return.

The air commanded
the scarlet and heroic blue in the veins.
Wings, wings heavenly and white, broken wings,
embattled wings without feathers chalked the field.

And the air had legs
and trunk and arms and head.

And all for you, Platko,
blond, Hungarian Platko!

And in your honor, for your return,
because you brought lost energy back to the fight,
the wind opened a path to the enemy's goal.

Nobody, nobody forgets.

The sky, the sea, the rain remember it.
The badges,
the gold badges, the boutonnieres,
are closed, but for you they will open.

No, nobody, nobody, nobody,
nobody forgets, Platko.

Not the end, your exit;
bloody blond bear,
pale flag, carried across the field on shoulders.

Oh Platko, Platko, Platko,
you, so far from Hungary!

What sea would not have been able to mourn you?

Nobody, nobody forgets,
no, nobody, nobody, nobody.

The Angel of Numbers

Virgins with rulers
and compasses were watching
the heavenly blackboards.

And the angel of numbers
was thoughtfully flying
from 1 to 2, from 2
to 3, from 3 to 4.

Cold chalk and sponges
streaked and erased
the light of the heavens.

There was no sun, no moon, no stars,
no sudden green
of lightning,
no air. Only mist.

Virgins without rulers,
without compasses were crying.

And on the dead blackboards
the angel of numbers
was lifeless, shrouded
on the 1 and the 2,
on the 3, on the 4 . . .

Song of the Luckless Angel

You are what moves:
water that carries me,
that will leave me.

Look for me in the wave.

What moves and doesn't return:
wind that in shadows
dies down and rises.

Look for me in the snow.

What nobody knows:
the floating earth
that speaks to nobody.

Look for me in the air.

The Moldy Angel

There was light that brought
for bone bitter almond.

Voice that for sound,
the fringe of rain
cut by an axe.

Soul that for body,
the bare sheath
of a two-edged sword.

Veins that for blood,
gall of myrrh and dyeweed.

Body that for soul,
emptiness, nothing.

The Angel of Ash

Once the lights were thrown
down by heavenly landslides
you came on a boat
of clouds, Angel of Ash.

You came to break chains
and match earth against wind.

You were blind with anger.

You came to break chains
and match sea against fire.

The world was battered around
and rolled through nothingness, dead.
Nobody knew what happened.
Just you and I, Angel of Ash.

The Good Angel

Inside my chest
huge hallways open
that swallow all seas.

Large windows
that light up all streets.

Rooftops
that bring closer all towers.

Deserted cities
suddenly come to life.
Trains that were derailed
couple and move on.

Old shipwrecks float again.
The light dips its foot in the water.

Bells!

The air spins faster.
The world, being the world,
fits in a child's hand.

Bells!

An angel brought down orders from heaven.

The Avaricious Angel

People on streetcorners
of towns and countries not on the map,
were whispering:

That man is dead
and doesn't know it.
He wants to break into the bank,
rob clouds, stars, gold comets,
and to buy what is hardest to get:
the sky.
And the man is dead.

Tremors shake his forehead.
Landslides,
confused echoes,
mingled sounds of picks and shovels,
in his ears.
In his eyes,
acetylene torches
and damp, golden corridors.
In his heart,
explosions of stone, outbursts of joy, dynamite.

He dreams of mines.

The Good Angel

The one I wanted came,
the one I called.

Not the one who sweeps away defenseless skies,
stars without homes,
moons without a country,
snows.
The kind of snows that fall from a hand,
a name,
a dream,
a face.

Not the one who tied death
to his hair.

The one I wanted.

Without scraping air,
without wounding leaves or shaking windowpanes.

The one who tied silence
to his hair.

To scoop out, without hurting me,
a shoreline of sweet light inside my chest
so that my soul could sail.

The Sleepwalking Angels

I

Consider that hour
when the invisible eyes of bedrooms
rebelled in the dark against a king.

You all know about it. Leave me alone!
If it happens that caves of snow
and tombs of stilled water
and clouds of oxidized dreams open beside me,
then lock up your eyelids forever.
What more do you want?

Large invisible eyes come at me.
Luminous spines sink into the walls.
Dead pupils roll back
and so do the sheets.

A king is a porcupine of eyelashes.

2

And that's not all.
There are also invisible ears in the bedrooms
fighting a king in the dark.

You know that my mouth is a well of names,
numbers and dead letters,
that echoes wither without my words,

that what I don't say despises and hates the wind.
There's nothing for you to hear.
Just leave me alone!

But ears grow against my chest,
cold ears of plaster,
they sink into my throat,
into the tubes of my bones,
into the heavy cellars of my blood.

A king is a porcupine without secrets.

Three Memories of Heaven

HOMAGE TO GUSTAVO ADOLFO BECQUER

ᘐ Prologue

Neither the rose nor the angel had been born.
It was before the bleating and weeping,
when light still didn't know
if the sea would be male or female,
when wind still dreamed of hair to comb
and fire dreamed of carnations and cheeks to burn
and water of lips set for drinking.
It was before the body, name and time.

It was then, I remember, that once in heaven . . .

ᘐ First Memory

   . . . a snapped lily . . .
   —G.A. BECQUER

She would walk with the air of a thoughtful lily
or a bird that knows it will be born.
She looked and did not see herself in the mirror her dream had made
     from the moon.
And she looked in the silence of snow that lifted her feet.
She was there in the silence.
It was before the harp or rain or words.
She didn't know.
White pupil of the air,
she trembled, green length and stem,
with stars, with flowers, and with trees;

with my stars
so unaware of everything
they drowned her in two seas
to carve two inlets in her eyes.

And I remember . . .

Nothing more: death, the fading away.

∿ *Second Memory*

> . . . the sound of kisses and
> the beating of wings . . .
> —G.A. BECQUER

It was also before,
long before burning feathers fell to earth
from the rebellion of shadows
and a bird could be killed by a lily.
It was even before you could ask me
the place and number of my body.
It was long before the body.
It was in the time of the soul.
It was when you uncovered the first dynasty of dreams
in the crownless forehead of heaven,
when you saw me in nothingness
and invented the first word.

It was then that we met.

Third Memory

. . . behind the fan of golden feathers . . .
—G.A. BECQUER

The waltzes of heaven had not yet wed jasmine and snow,
nor had the wind considered the possible music of your hair,
nor had the king decreed the violet be buried in a book.
No.
It was a time when the swallow travelled
without our initials on its beak,
when bellflowers and bindweeds
died without balconies to climb and stars.
It was a time
when no flower leaned its head on the shoulder of a bird.

It was then, behind your fan, we found our first moon.

The Angel of Sand

It is true, in your eyes the sea was two boys staring at me,
afraid of harsh words and of being trapped,
two terrible boys of the night, thrown out of heaven,
whose childhoods were a robbing of boats and crimes of suns and
     moons.
Close your eyes and try to sleep.

I saw that the real sea was a boy who leaped naked,
inviting me in for a dish of stars and a nap of seaweed.
Yes. Yes. My life was going to be, and already was, a shore set adrift.
But when you woke up, you drowned me in your eyes.

The Bad Moment

In the days when I used to think
that fields of wheat were the homes of stars and gods
and frost a gazelle's frozen tears,
somebody whitewashed my chest and my shadow,
and I was betrayed.

It was a moment of bullets gone wild,
of the sea's making off with men who wished to be birds,
of the telegram bringing bad news and the finding of blood,
of the death of the water that always had stared at the sky.

The Grade-School Angels

None of us understood the dark secret of the blackboards
nor why the armillary sphere seemed so remote when we looked at it.
We knew only that a circumference does not have to be round
and that an eclipse of the moon confuses the flowers
and speeds up the timing of birds.

None of us understood anything:
not even why our fingers were made of India ink
and the afternoon closed compasses only to have the dawn open
        books.
We knew only that a straight line, if it likes, can be curved or broken
and that the wandering stars are children who don't know arithmetic.

Living Snow

Without lying, what a lie of snow walked mutely through my dream,
voiceless snow, blue-eyed perhaps, slow and with long hair.
When did it shake out the curls of fire with its blank stares?
Mutely it walked, whitening questions no one could answer,
whitening tombs, erased and forgotten, in order to begin new memories,
giving to ashes, already in air, the shape of boneless light.

Invitation to the Harp

1

Go far, far away.
To rooms where gloves that have turned to dust are being forgotten,
where pier glasses dream of eyelids and names long gone,
where a hat is bored
and barrettes without curls grow weary,
where if violets tire
it's because they're nostalgic for moiré and fans.

Go even farther away.
To rooms where leaks in the ceiling
open their damp maps so that sofas might travel,
where springs collapse without hope
and invisible faces leave streaks on the mirrors.

Go to the land of cobwebs.

2

Go even farther away than that.
Where the moon is torn between a poplar leaf and a passionate book,
where there are midnight frosts that candelabra conceal
and where death shivers in the unsteady sleep of the candles,
where a puppet in mourning dies over a tuberose,
where a voice from oblivion stirs the sleeping water of pianos.

Go always farther away, farther away.
Go where floors retain the echoes and shadows of footsteps,
where moths watch over the silence of neckties,
where a hundred years is a harp that has been forgotten.

The False Angel

So that I might walk among tangles of roots
and the bone houses of worms,
that I might hear the creaking of the world
and seize with my teeth the stone light of a star,
you pitched your tent west of my sleep, False Angel.

You people joined by the same current of water,
bound by an act of betrayal and the fall of a star,
look at me, listen to me, take shelter in the lost voices of ruins.
Hear the stones toll out the hours of their dying.

Don't let go of each other.

There are spiders that die without homes
and ivy that bursts into flame and rains blood when brushed by a
    shoulder
and lizards whose skeletons shine in the moonlight.
If you can remember heaven,
the fury of cold will stand up in the thistles,
in the seemingly innocent ditches that strangle
the dawn's one pleasure, the birds.
Whoever thinks always about the living will see clay molds
lived in by faithless, tireless angels,
sleepwalking angels keeping track of the orbits of weariness.

Why keep on going?
Dampness and broken glass are good friends
and after a nightmare the frost wakens nails
and scissors and freezes the mourning of ravens.

It's all over.
You can be proud of yourself, False Angel, for the faded tails of dying
     comets,
for killing a man already dead,
for weeping a tireless stream of tears over a shadow,
for smothering the air in its last breath.

The Dead Angels

You must look for them
in the sleeplessness of forgotten pipes,
in sewers clogged by the silence of garbage.
They are not far from puddles over which clouds move without
        stopping,
nor far from a broken ring,
a trampled star,
some lost eyes.

I know because I have seen them
in those heaps of rubbish that appear in the mist,
because I have touched them
in the no man's land of a dead brick
come to nothing from a building or cart.
They are never far from chimneys that fall
or from leaves that will cling to a shoe forever.

All that may be.
But they also exist in those splinters which burn without fire,
in those crushing desertions that pieces of broken-down furniture
        suffer,
and they are not ever far from the names and signs that are frozen on
        walls.

You must look for them
under the drop of wax that buries a word in a book
or the name at the end of a letter
that lies gathering dust.
Look for them

near a lost bottlecap,
near a shoe gone astray in the snow,
near a razorblade left at the edge of a cliff.

The Surviving Angel

Remember.
The snow brought drops of sealing-wax and molten lead
and the lies of a little girl who had killed a swan,
and a gloved hand brought the dispersion of light and the murder
that seemed to go on forever,
and a friend brought about the downfall of heaven.

Remember that day, remember
and do not forget the pulse and color of stars stiffened with surprise,
and in the cold two phantoms died,
and a bird found three gold rings
which it buried in frost;
it was the day when the last cry of a man bloodied the wind,
when all the angels lost their lives
except for one, and he was left wounded, unable to fly.

They Have Gone

They are the leaves,
leaves destroyed because they wanted to live forever,
because they didn't want to think for six moons about what makes a
      wasteland,
because they didn't want to know why a drop of water insists on hitting a
      naked skull already nailed to bad weather.
Other disgraces could occur to us.
What's the date today?

The leaves sweep themselves into piles with the bones that in life never
      acquired rights to a tomb.
I know that I hurt you,
that there is no place to escape to,
that the blood in my veins has suffered a seizure of smoke.
You had yellow eyes and now you obviously can't understand that they're
      ashes.

We *are* not.
We *were* this or that.

That Burning Horse in the Lost Forests

(ELEGY FOR FERNANDO VILLALON 1881–1930)

It has been proven, the horror of a pair of stiff shoes against the last
      board of a box destined to stave off
a short while the invasion of earth,
the earth that hears what it knows about heaven by listening to roots,
the earth that seems to gather in light only when wounded by picks,
cut up by shovels,
or clawed by beasts and birds that prefer the sleep of the dead force
      the moon to set over graves of blood.
Leave the flat roofs alone,
avoid the slamming of doors and the cries of a child for whom clothes
      in a corner are shifting phantoms.
What do you know about any of this,
about what happens when a head slumps down on the broadest of
      shoulders or about what happens when a nail in shadow loosens
      the dustiest sigh from a forgotten guitar?
What does it matter to you that a lonely sword jumps from one poplar
      to another or that a fiery banderilla flies from the left bank of a
      brook and turns the bittern's cry to stone?
Only I understand these things
and what is more, at eleven-twenty in the morning.

It seems like only yesterday.

And that this was somebody buried with a silver watch in his lower
      vest pocket,
which meant that at one the islands would vanish,
and at two the heads of the blackest bulls would turn white,
and at three a lead bullet would pierce the lonely host left out in the
      reliquary of a church lost at the crossing of two paths: one going
      to a whorehouse, the other to a health resort

(and the watch on the dead man),
which meant that at four the swollen river carrying the skeleton of a fish
      hooked to the pantleg of a foreign sailor would flow past a reed,
and at five a toad lost among vegetables in a garden would be cut in two
      by the unexpected entry of a wheel from a cart capsized in a ditch,
and at six some unhappy cows would hurl themselves against the caboose
      of an express train,
and at seven some men on a street corner would stab a drunken girl
      stepping outside her door to throw clamshells and olive pits into
      the street
(and the watch on the dead man),
which meant that at eight five cats with cropped ears would knock over
      the vinegar and hallway mirrors would crack with anguish,
and at nine in the deserted sand of the bullring an invisible hand would
      mark the spot where at 4:07 in the afternoon a banderillero would
      be gored to death,
and at ten no matches would light for a weeping woman in a dark
      hallway and northwest of a lost island a tanker would see the eyes
      of all the drowned pass by
(and the watch on the dead man),
which meant that at eleven two friends in different parts of the world
      would mistakenly enter the wrong house and be shot to death on
      the nineteenth step of a stair,
which meant that at twelve my own blood would freeze and with my
      eyes wide open I would suddenly find myself in a well lit only by
      luminous fumes rising from the thigh bones of a child buried
      beside a vein of limestone more than fifty feet below sea-level.

Yes. Yes.

Here is where one leaves for deserted planets,
for yellow ponds where frozen words that could never be spoken by the
      living float like smoke.
Here the strongest echoes despair.

I have lost my horse.

But it's because I come from half-open doors,

from dark places where the worst crimes are being plotted with soft
voices,

from lofts where hands go numb on suddenly finding the reason for
the wasting away of a whole family.

Yes,

but I have lost my horse

and my body walks through the southwest looking for me

and today the train arrives two thousand years late

and I don't know who has burned these olive trees.

Goodbye.

Two Children

I

Now you need only wait for the appearance of those hidden springs
that lead to the narrow hallways where light is discouraged by signs of
     death.
A spirit who still values the earth a little asks you,
Won't heaven be scared by the untimeliness of your journey?

Don't those narrow hallways that lead to the winter of a courtyard
freeze the anguish of eternity that hisses through your blood?
Doesn't the open skylight, suffering because it takes in the pain of a
     cloud,
kill in your eyelids any desire for hours without end?
It is early,
much too early for a child to be left to the shadows.

2

You can easily see that the night considers a boy differently
than the day which drowns him in a drop of water.
What does the swallow know of the owl's insomnia?

For God's sake,
kill him without the dawn's having to guess if it will happen or not.

He has left his head forgotten between two wires.
He has shouted his heart out so that echoes would turn against him.
Ask the needles that have been lost in sofas for his hands.

Where is that boy going who makes wrong turns?

Fragments of a Wish

... That when air is disloyal to the straightness of lilies,
it be sentenced to die by whirling water;
that the shadow of sorrow need not be what trees push toward the
     west;
that the forest ranger tell you who pays for the cold;

that if in your country all hope is lost in the long heat of summer,
the snows in my country help you to get it back;
that if the tread of a shoe doesn't have time to put a violet to sleep,
you spend your life here, culling the cycles of rain.

It is sad,
very sad to know that a hand stamped in dust
lasts a shorter time than it takes a leaf to face up to its death.

Isn't it painful when those threads suddenly die against your cheeks,
when emptied from clouds they freeze in pools?

That's the Way It Is

More fallen each time,
more distant from surfaces punished by the feet of soldiers,
farther away from those with soft voices who lean over my shoulders,
     wanting to hold me in check as if I were a shifting piece of earth.
I see my blood beside my body
that fell like a freezing whirlwind.
And this tongue,
this throat now ready to stifle that drop of water one hears in every
     goodbye,
this tongue and this throat that have made the world so boring to me,
I wish they would go away and not tell me about it.

There below,
lost in the light that treats me just like another corpse among the tombs,
next to the danger of names that are turning to dust,
there with the distant sadness of those who cannot speak of their travels,
to the right and left of those too much alone I wait for you.

Charlie's Sad Date

My necktie, my gloves.
My gloves, my necktie.

The butterfly knows nothing about the death of the tailors,
about wardrobes conquering the sea.
Gentlemen, my age is 900,000 years.
Wow!

I was a boy when fish didn't swim,
when geese didn't say mass
or the snail attack the cat.
Miss, let's play at cat and mouse.

The saddest thing, mister, is a watch:
11, 12, 1, 2.

At three on the dot a passerby will drop dead.
You, moon, moon of late taxis,
smokey moon of firemen,
don't be scared.

The city is burning in the sky,
clothing like mine gets sick of the country.
My age is suddenly 25.

Because it snows, it snows
and my body turns into a wooden shack.
Wind, I invite you to rest.
It is too late to dine on stars.

But we can dance, lost tree,
a waltz for wolves,
for the sleep of the hen without fox's claws.

I have mislaid my cane.
It is very sad to think of it alone in the world.
My cane!

My hat, my cuffs,
my gloves, my shoes.

The bone that hurts most, my love, is the watch:
11, 12, 1, 2.

3 on the dot.
In the pharmacy a nude cadaver evaporates.

Harold Lloyd, Student

Do you have the umbrella?
Avez-vous le parapluie?

No, sir, I do not have the umbrella.
Non, monsieur, je n'ai pas le parapluie.

Alice, I have the hippopotamus.
L'hippopotame for you.
Avez-vous le parapluie?

Oui.
Sí.
Yes.

That, which, who, whose.
If the she-lizard is my friend,
then clearly the he-beetle is your friend.
Was it your fault that it rained?
No, the rain was not your fault.
Alice, Alice, it was my fault,
I who study for you
and for this unknowing fly, flowering nightingale of my glasses.

29, 28, 27, 26, 25, 24, 23, 22.
$2\pi r$, πr^2
and converted itself into the mule, Nebuchadnezzar,
and your soul and mine into a royal bird of paradise.

Fish no longer sing in the Nile
nor does the moon set for the dahlias of the Ganges.

Alice,
why do you love me with that sad crocodile air
and the deep pain of a quadratic equation?

Le printemps pleut sur Les Anges.

The Spring rains over Los Angeles
in that sad hour when the police
are unaware of the suicide of the isosceles triangles,
the melancholy of a Naperian logarithm
and the *facial unibusquibusque.*

In that sad hour when the moon becomes almost equal
to the whole misfortune
of this love of mine multiplied by X
and to the wings of the afternoon that fold
over an acetylene flower
or a bird of gas.

Of this my pure love so delicately idiotic.
Quousque tandem abutere Catilina patientia nostra?

So sweet and deliberately idiotic,
capable of making the square of a circle cry
and obliging that fool, Mr. Nequaqua Schmitt,
to sell at public auction those stars that belong to the river
and those blue eyes that skyscrapers open to me.

Alice, Alice, my love!
Alice, Alice, my nanny!
Follow me by bicycle through the air
even though the police may not know astronomy,
the secret police.

Even though the police may not know that a sonnet
consists of two quatrains
and two tercets.

Buster Keaton Looks in the Woods for His Love Who Is a Real Cow

1, 2, 3, 4,
My shoes don't fit in these four tracks.
If my shoes don't fit in these four tracks,
whose tracks are they?
A shark's?
A new-born elephant's? A duck's?
A flea's? A quail's?

(Yooo Hooo)

Georginaaaaaaaa!
Where are you?
I don't hear you, Georgina!
What will your father's mustache think of me?

(PaaaPaaaaa)

Georginaaaaaaaa!
Are you here or not?

Spruce, where is she?
Alder, where is she?
Pine, where is she?

Has Georgina come by here?

(Yooo Hooo, Yooo Hooo.)

She came by at one, munching grass.
Caw caw,

the crow was leading her on with some mignonette.
Wooo wooo,
the owl with a dead mouse.

Excuse me, gentlemen, but it makes me want to cry!
(Booo hooo, booo hooo.)
Georgina!
Now you are short only one horn
of acquiring a postman's cap and a doctorate
in the truly useful profession of cyclist.

(Cri, cri, cri, cri.)

Even the crickets pity me
and the tick shares my sorrow.
Pity him in the tuxedo who looks for you and cries for you
in one rainstorm after another,
the soft-hearted one, the one in the derby,
who worries about you among the trees.

Georginaaaaaaaaaaaaaaaaaa!

(Mooooooooooooooo.)

Are you a sweet child or a real cow?
My heart always told me that you were a real cow.
Your father, that you were a sweet child.
My heart, that you were a real cow.
A sweet child.
A real cow.
A child.
A cow.
A child or a cow?
Or a child and a cow?

I never found out.
        Goodbye, Georgina.
                (Bang!)

On the Day of His Death by an Armed Hand

Come right out and tell me if those weren't the good old days.
5 × 5 was not yet 25
nor had the dawn considered the pointless existence of knives gone
    dull.

I swear to you by the moon I won't be a cook,
you swear to me by the moon you won't be a cook,
he swears to us by the moon he won't even be smoke in such a sad
    kitchen.

Who died?

The goose is sorry for being a duck,
the sparrow for being a professor of Chinese,
the rooster for being a man,
and I for having talent and marvelling at how miserable
the sole of a shoe usually is in winter.

A queen has lost her crown,
a president of a republic his hat,
and I . . .

        I believe that I have lost nothing,
        that I have never lost anything,
        that I . . .

        What does buenos días mean?

Metamorphosis of the Carnation

TO RICARDO E. MOLINARI

I

By the sea and a river and in my early years,
I wanted to be a horse.

The shores of rushes were made of wind and mares.
I wanted to be a horse.

Their high-arching tails brushed the stars.
I wanted to be a horse.

At the beach, Mother, listen to my slow-paced trot.
I wanted to be a horse.

After tomorrow, Mother, I shall live by the sea.
I wanted to be a horse.

A four-legged girl sleeps in its depths.
I wanted to be a horse.

2

What do I have in my hand?
(I hope it turns into a shell for you.)

What do I have in my hand?
(I hope it turns into a tree for you.)

What do I have in my hand?
(I hope it turns into leaves for you.)

What do I have in my hand?
(I hope it turns into a tuberose for you.)

3

The horse asked for sheets
that were rippled like rivers,
sheets that were white.

"I want to be a man just for one night.
You can call me at dawn."

The woman did not call him.
(He never went back to his stable.)

4

The dove made a mistake.
It was mistaken.

To go north it went south.
It thought that wheat was water.
It was mistaken.

It thought that the sea was the sky,
that night was morning.

It was mistaken.
That stars were dew,
that fire was snow.
It was mistaken.

That your skirt was your blouse,
that your heart was its home.
It was mistaken.

(It slept on the shore,
and you in the high branch of a tree.)

5

At dawn the rooster was shaken.

His echo came back to him
in a boy's voice.

The rooster
found masculine signs.

The rooster was shaken.

With eyes full of love and battles,
he leaped to an orange tree.
From the orange tree to a lemon tree,
from the lemon tree to a courtyard,
from the courtyard to a bedroom,
went the rooster.

The woman who was sleeping there
embraced him.

The rooster was shaken.

6

The cow
in the field.

"I want to be the lady of the house."

The man
in his room.

"I want to be a bull in the field."

(Where their wishes crossed,
A blushing child leaped up.)

7

"Love!" screeched the parrot.
(No answer from the poplars.)

"My love, my love!"
(Silence in the pines.)

"Looove!"
(No sound from the river either.)

"I am dying!"
(The poplar,
the pine,
the river,
none of them went to his funeral.)

To Luis Cernuda: Looking for Southern Air in England

Suppose the air said to itself one day:
>   I am tired,
dead tired of my name . . . I no longer want
even my initial to sign the carnation's curl,
the rose's ripple,
the river's fine folds,
the sea's graceful flowing and the dimple
that laughs in the sail's cheek . . .

I rise from the soft,
slumbering surfaces
housing my sleep.
I flow from hanging vines, I slip through
the blind, arched-windows of towers;
already thinness itself, I turn
sharp-cornered streets, entering,
broken and wounded by doorways,
long halls that lead to green patios
where jetting water, sweet and hopeless,
reminds me of what I wish for . . .

I look and look for a name for myself,
but I don't know how.
Isn't there any breeze, or breath
able to lift into view
the word that would name me?

More and more tired, I look for a sign,
a something or someone to take my place,

who would be like me and live like me
in the fresh memory of things, who would
be moved by cradle and cradlesong,
who would endure with the same
trembling, the same breath
that was mine the first morning
of my life when light said to me:
"Fly. You are the air."

Suppose the air said to itself one day . . .

Going Back to a Birthday

J . R . J .

That afternoon I climbed
with my first poems
to the lonely rooftop
where he glowed in the silence
among honeysuckle and jasmine.
I brought him stanzas
about the sea and sailors,
yellow dunes,
the clear indigo of shadows
and walls of fresh lime
figured with fountains and gardens.
I also brought him
his school afternoons,
sad hours of study,
colored maps,
the baby-blue of atlases,
melancholy blackboards
white from the suffering of numbers.
I used to climb that bough
of tender, joyful, brief
everyday happenings
with the same trembling
I felt when I climbed
the astonished tree
that protected me once
when I wanted to reach
the lightning rods on the tower.
Like a candle
burning at twilight,
he would lean on the railing

open to the mountains,
their snow spared
by the brown hand of June.
We spoke with passion
of our sea, the way one would
of an absent friend
he has not seen for many years
and wished to be with constantly.
When night entered
and I could hardly see him,
his dark voice was there,
or maybe the shadow
of his voice,
still speaking of the sea,
of the sea as if
he might not see it again.
Fateful time!
He was then
the same age that I am today,
December sixteenth,
here, so far
from that pure afternoon
when I took him the sea
up to his lonely rooftop.

Going Back Through Color

Colors calm you this afternoon: green
shows up like a child of spring,
in the windows a clear sea of sky changes
the smiling wing of a blue homing pigeon.

The proud and trembling whites
that daisies open against the vines make you go back,
and so does the ivory of the magnolia's budding breasts,
and the snow-white of footprints over the pond.

You think of the distant colors of other days:
that blue asleep on its back on the marshes,
the gold of stones fallen beside
the ancient teeth of the sea they worship.

In the pink of the rosebush you listen for the pink
falling from roses torn up behind the balcony of the harp,
and in the bright black of shadows, you see the luster
of the dead hats of tall grandfathers.

Don't lose the colors that open paths for you
in your small walled garden this afternoon. Look.
Here they are. Touch them. They are the same colors
that live in your heart, a little faded now.

The Coming Back of Love in Bright Landscapes

We believe, my love, that those landscapes
have remained asleep or dead with whatever we were
in the times, in the days, when we inhabited them;
we believe that trees lose their memory
and that nights pass, giving to oblivion
what made them beautiful and maybe immortal.

But the slightest trembling of a leaf
or the sudden breathing of a faded star is enough
for us to have the same joys those places
filled us with and gave us together.
And so today, my love, you waken at my side
among the currants and hidden strawberries
sheltered by the constant heart of the woods.

There is the damp caress of dew,
the delicate grasses that cool your bed,
the charmed sylphs that adorn your long hair
and the high mysterious squirrels that rain
the small green of branches upon your sleep.

Leaf, be happy always; you that have brought me
with your slight trembling
the aroma of such blind luminous days,
may you never know autumn.
And you, smallest of lost stars that opens for me
the intimate windows of my earliest nights,
never shut off your light
over all the bedrooms we slept in till dawn,

nor in the moonlit library,
nor over those books in sweet disorder,
nor over the mountains outside awake and singing to us.

The Coming Back of Love on the Sands

This morning, love, we are twenty years old.
Slowly, of their own free will,
our barefoot shadows entwine, walking
from the orchards that face the sea's blue with their greens.
You are still almost the same vision
that came one lightless evening between two lights
when a young man, lost in thought, made sure
to take the long way home from town.
You are still the one at my side,
searching for the secret incline of the dunes,
the hidden slope of sand, the concealed
reeds that form
shades before the sea eyes of the wind.
There you are, and there I am beside you, checking
the high temperature of the happy waves,
the sea's heart blindly risen,
and dying in bits of sweet salt and spindrift.
And later, on the shore, everything looks at us joyfully.
The fallen castles lift their battlements,
seaweed offers us crowns, and sails,
bellied in flight, want to sing over the towers.

This morning, love, we are twenty years old.

Facing the Spanish Coast

(FROM THE "FLORIDA")

Beautiful mother, so sad and yesterday so happy, today
you show me your wrinkled face in the morning
as I pass before you still powerless,
after so much time, even to embrace you.
You rise from the stars of the Mediterranean
night, frowning with mist,
strong, bound, huge and painful.
Snow can be seen on your high hair
of Granada, stained forever
with the pure blood that cradled you
and sang to you—oh mountains!—so happy.
I don't want to take you from my eyes,
from my heart, mother, not for one moment
as you become visible, far off, to look at me.
I give you my steady gaze, I watch you
over the slow waves of this boat,
from this deck that passes and carries me
again far away from your love, my mother.
This is my sea, the dream of my childhood
of sand, of dolphins and seagulls.
Your people secretly leave you, they break
from your sweet coastal skin,
your face white as chalk, streaked
with wounds and shadows of your heroes.
Along here joy fled with terror.
Over this long and hard side
you sink into the surf,
the suffering went from Málaga to Almería,
the pitiless crime,
still—shamelessly—unpunished.

I wish you would look at me passing today joyful
the same as when long ago
I was inside you,
schoolboy or soldier,
voice of your people, singing passionate and free
of your bloodstained,
green and high shaken crowns.
Say goodbye, mother, the way I do,
almost without saying it, goodbye, so that now,
once more there is only sea and sky by themselves,
I can live again, if you command it,
die, die also, if that's what you want.

The Coming Back of an Assassinated Poet

You have come back to me older and sadder in the drowsy
light of a quiet dream in March, your dusty temples
disarmingly gray, and that olive
bronze you had in your magical youth,
furrowed by the passing of years, just as if
you lived out slowly in death
the life you never had while you were alive.

I do not know what you wanted to tell me tonight
with your unexpected visit, the fine alpaca
suit, looking like new, the yellow tie,
and your carefully combed hair suffering the wind, the same as
when you walked through those gardens of poplars
and hot oleanders of our schooldays.

Maybe you thought—I want to explain myself
now that I stand outside the dream—that you
had to come first to me from those buried
roots or hidden springs where
your bones despair.
                Tell me,
tell me,
if in the mute embrace you have given me,
in the tender gesture of offering me a chair, in the simple
manner of sitting near me, of looking at me,
smiling and in silence, without a single word,
tell me if you did not mean
that in spite of our minor disagreements,
you remain joined to me more than ever in death

for the times perhaps
we were not—oh, forgive me!—in life.

If this is not true, come back again in a dream
some other night to tell me so.

The Coming Back of Vicente Aleixandre

(1958)

Where are you, my friend,
where are you coming from, from what depth
of years do you come to me
this noon so far
from those other noons or those nights
in which I would meet you,
tall, trim, and blond,
as if you were already looking for what would give you
with time that voice in which
the freshness of those days still breathes?

Things have happened. Shadowy seas,
black curtains, have fallen.
A rapid collapse of clouds
has drowned us and buried
even some of our precious blood.
Listen to them as I listen to them, here, so far away,
so far that with my hands I can, at times,
touch the sound . . .
              Yes, things have happened,
many things. But look:
death always recedes, always
its stiff waves let the painful light pass
where life begins, happy child of blue foam.

And so now, my friend,
in this distant noon
of sun high in the treetops swaying
with birds and sky
and those empty spaces

that have been part of me a long time, you come back
once more, refreshed and young,
as if so many past years
had been only one day,
a day without shadows.
                    May your future suns
not die and may they keep on
passing through you always
with the same motion so that in my memory
the light you have can talk to me.

Song

The swamps of Paraná!
A man on a balcony watches
the wind that comes and goes.

He sees the moving hollows
of the wind that comes and goes.

The horses that are like stones
of the wind that comes and goes.

The pastures like the green sea
of the wind that comes and goes.

The river like a wide sail
of the wind that comes and goes.

The ships that are like roads
of the wind that comes and goes.

The man that is like the shadow
of the wind that comes and goes.

The sky that is like the home
of the wind that comes and goes.

The man sees all that he looks at
and sees only himself alone.

Ballad of What the Wind Said

Eternity might very well
be only a river,
be a horse forgotten
and the cooing
of a lost dove.

As for the man who leaves
his fellow men, the wind comes
telling him other things,
opens his ears
and eyes to other things.

Today I left my fellow men
and alone in this ravine
began to look at the river
and saw a horse alone
and listened lonely
to the cooing
of a lost dove.

And then the wind came close
and like someone in passing
told me:
Eternity might very well
be only a river,
be a horse forgotten
and the cooing
of a lost dove.

Song

The ships pass so close
to the shore
that they could well take
a branch from the willows
that grow on the shore.

So close is the shore
that ships if they wanted
could also take
a horse from the shore.

It's good to be at the edge
of this shore
where ships can,
if ships really want,
carry to sea a horse,
a willow branch
and even the shore.

Song

A balcony over a river,
a few horses grazing,
are all that is needed
to go on a voyage
night and day
without moving at all.

The horses are very still,
the river is always quiet.
Once in awhile
a ship will pass,
disturbing the scene,
and the air in order to stir
and do some work
moves one of the horses over
and leaves him there.

The man on the balcony meanwhile
has come back from a very long trip
without having moved at all.

Ballad of the Country Idlers

They are sitting and looking.
Not doing a thing.

They are twenty or thirty years old.
And they are sitting and looking.

What are they looking at?
                    They're looking at nothing.
What are they listening to?
                    They're listening to nothing.
What do they talk about when they talk,
not doing a thing?
Boredom has placed
loneliness on their faces;
their foreheads are peaceful
and their hands always limp
which is why that motionless stone
sits on their faces.

There is no news. And waves
from the world barely reach them.
And if they reach them, they don't listen.
And if they listen, they hear nothing.

They are less than those horses
and cows
grazing together and looking
from time to time at the river,
neighing and lowing
from time to time.

They are less than the bleating
sheep,
than the hummingbird sucking
flowers for them,
than the windmill bringing up
water for them,
than those thieves passing by
robbing fruit trees for them.
They are less than the thieves
passing by.

They keep on sitting and looking.
Not doing a thing.
Other hands have already gotten
tired for them.
And now, they rest.
Sitting, they rest.

Ballad of the Lost Andalusian

Lost is the Andalusian
on the other side of the river.

"River that knows him,
who is he and why did he come?"

He might have seen olive trees
by the banks of another river.

"River that knows him,
what is he doing always along your shores?"

He might have seen hatred and war
by the banks of another river.

"River that knows him,
what does he do alone on your shores?"

I see his little house
on the other side of the river.

I don't see the olive trees
on the other side of the river.

Only horses, horses, horses,
all of them lost and alone.

The loneliness of an Andalusian
on the other side of the river.

What will he do this Andalusian
on the other side of the river?

Song

A thistle flowered
and the field lit up.

Horses caught fire.
Everything burned.

Cows of light grazed
in the bright pastures.

Out of the river
boats of sun sailed.

Out of my heart
another heart blazed.

Song

There was a river
that one day at noon
turned into steel.
Ships that went by on it
never came back.
Only the wind did, only the wind.

The furious wind, all at once,
tried to break through it.
With its head and its breast.
Day and night,
with its head and its breast.

But the river was a river
of steel.
Now and forever of steel.

Notes to Rafael Alberti

PLATKO

Alberti notes in his autobiography, *La Arboleda Perdida,* ". . . suddenly, leaving to one side wings and darkness [he was then at work on "Three Memories of Heaven"], I wrote an ode to a soccer player—Platko—heroic goalie in a game between Real of San Sebastian and Barcelona." Platko played for Barcelona.

THREE MEMORIES OF HEAVEN

Gustavo Adolfo Becquer (1836–1870) was the author of only one book of poems, but is considered by many to be Spain's most important nineteenth-century poet.

THAT BURNING HORSE IN THE LOST FORESTS

Fernando Villalon was an Andalusian poet and friend of Lorca's and Alberti's. It was his last wish to be buried with his watch running.

METAMORPHOSIS OF THE CARNATION

I have chosen seven of the eighteen poems that make up the original work. Ricardo Molinari was an Argentine poet (1898–1996).

TO LUIS CERNUDA: LOOKING FOR SOUTHERN AIR IN ENGLAND

Luis Cernuda (1904–1963), Sevillian-born poet of the "Generation of 1927." At the time of this poem (1942) he was living in England.

GOING BACK TO A BIRTHDAY

J.R.J. is Juan Ramón Jiménez, the great Andalusian poet and strong influence on Alberti and others of the "Generation of 1927." He had gone to the same Jesuit school as Alberti.

THE COMING BACK OF AN ASSASSINATED POET

The poet referred to in this poem is Federico García Lorca.

THE COMING BACK OF VICENTE ALEIXANDRE (1898–1984),

one of the "Generation of 1927" who continued to live in Spain.

A Note About the Author

Mark Strand was born in Summerside, Prince Edward Island, Canada, and was raised and educated in the United States. He has written nine books of poems, which have brought him many honors and grants, including a MacArthur Fellowship and the 1999 Pulitzer Prize for his book of poems *Blizzard of One*. He was chosen as Poet Laureate of the United States in 1990. He is the author of a book of stories, *Mr. and Mrs. Baby*, several volumes of translations (including these works by Rafael Alberti and Carlos Drummond de Andrade), the editor of a number of anthologies, and author of two monographs on contemporary artists. He teaches in the Committee on Social Thought at the University of Chicago.

A Note on the Type

This book was set in Janson, a typeface long thought to have been made by the Dutchman Anton Janson, who was a practicing typefounder in Leipzig during the years 1668–1687. However, it has been conclusively demonstrated that these types are actually the work of Nicholas Kis (1650–1702), a Hungarian, who most probably learned his trade from the master Dutch typefounder Dirk Voskens. The type is an excellent example of the influential and sturdy Dutch types that prevailed in England up to the time William Caslon (1692–1766) developed his own incomparable designs from them.

Composed by Creative Graphics, Allentown, Pennsylvania
Printed and bound by Edwards Brothers,
Ann Arbor, Michigan
Designed by Anthea Lingeman